shake, rattle & read!

IN THE SKY

Written by
Madeline Tyler

Illustrated by
Amy Li

BookLife
PUBLISHING

©2019
BookLife Publishing Ltd.
King's Lynn
Norfolk, PE30 4LS

ISBN: 978-1-78637-747-0

Written by:
Madeline Tyler

Edited by:
John Wood

Illustrated by:
Amy Li

To find out how to read this book, turn to the back cover.

All images and videos courtesy of Shutterstock. With thanks to Getty Images, Thinkstock Photo and iStockphoto.

Cover – KateChe, YamabikaY, Toluk, flovie, Ellika, masher, Ann.and.Pen, exile_artist, Fears. Recurring backgrounds – YamabikaY. Recurring texture brushes – Toluk (grunge), flovie (spotty), Anna Timoshenko (rock cracks). 4–7 –Dolka, Incomible, EV-DA, 8–11 –Iveta Angelova, mexico70, nubenamo, Katerina Pereverzeva, 12–15 –PinkPueblo, nubenamo, Ursa Major, Karbo_Kreto, 16–19 – Amma Shams, ekler, Fears, Karbo_Kreto, Ms Moloko, nubenamo, Natykach Nataliia, Ursa Major, 20–23 –Anna Timoshenko, masher, PixieMe.

Can you use your imagination to take a trip into the sky?

Follow the

INSTRUCTIONS

on each page and see what you can find.

There is a **butterfly** hiding in the leaves.

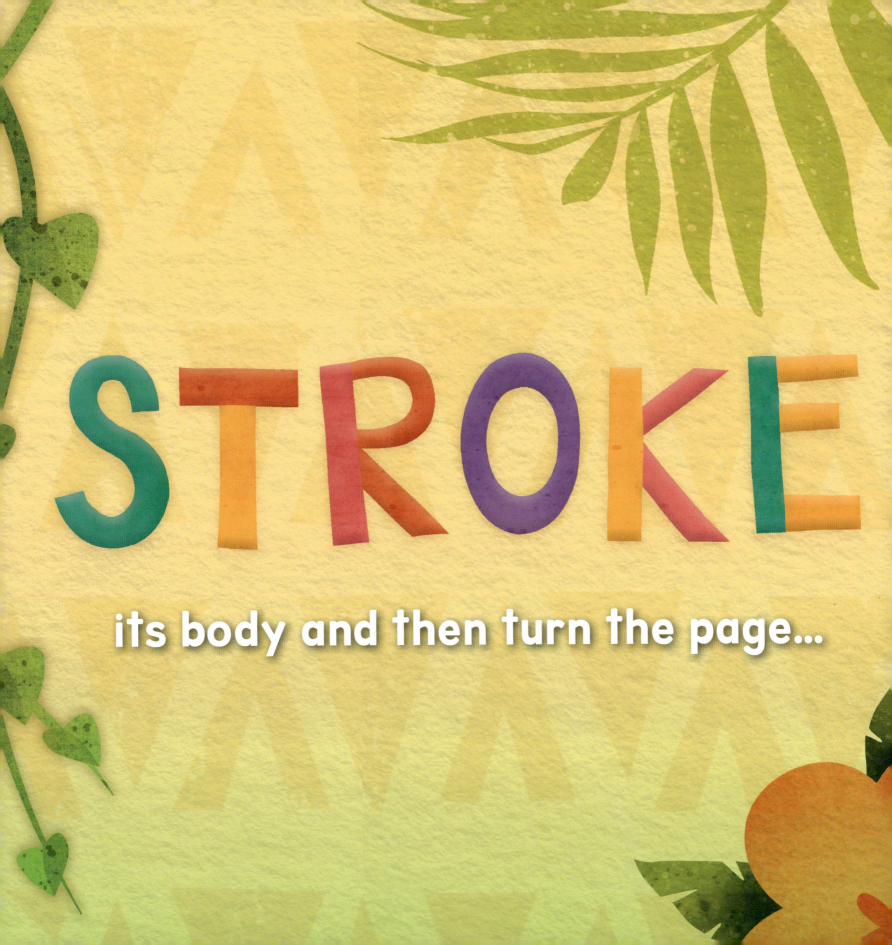

STROKE

its body and then turn the page...

Now its wings are open!

Look!

It is a **peacock!**

the book and turn the page.

What do you think will happen?

Wow! Those feathers
are very colourful!

Can you see the **sugar glider** in the tree?

BLOW

on the page to help it glide.

There it goes!

What bird is sitting up there?

Can you

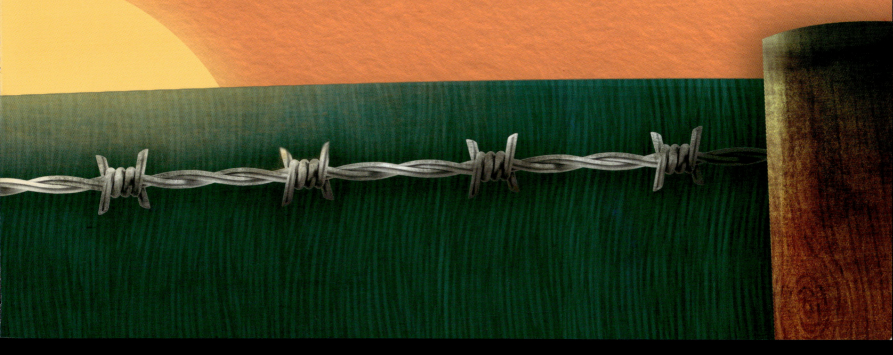

TAP

its head to make it turn around?

It is an
owl!

It is time for this **bat** to go to bed.

Spin this book

UPSIDE
DOWN

and turn the page...

Shh!

The bat has gone to sleep.

What colours can you see?